Poetic Keys... to the Kingdom!

Poetic Keys...
to the Kingdom!

"The Trinity Tablets"

Charles E. Dickerson

Neo Nexus Publishing, LLC

P.O. Box 3162

Irmo, South Carolina 29063

NeoNexusPublishing@Gmail.com

*

ISBN-10: 0-98466-733-4
ISBN-13: 978-0-98466-733-8
Library of Congress Control Number: 2014915452

*

Copyright © Charles E. Dickerson 2 0 1 4
First Edition
All Rights Reserved.

No part of this publication is to be reproduced in any manner without prior written permission from the publisher.

*

Printed in the United States of America.

Poetic Keys to the Kingdom!

Contents

Dedication	vii
Preface	viii
King of kings, Lord of lords	xi

~ First Trinity ~

The Shortest Poem Ever Written	2
The Scribe	3
The Precious Present	5
My Name Is Spirit	8
Rich Little	10
Thou Shall Not	11
Daughters	14
I Am That I Am	15
Divine Purpose	17
Seven Seals	19
Babylon	20
Mother Love	21
Cradle Of Hope	23
So They Say	24
The Seer	26
Thy Kingdom Come	28
You Are	29
God Knows	31

Poetic Keys to the Kingdom!

~ Second Trinity ~

The Greatest Name Ever Spoken	35
The Adam Family	36
Thank You Jesus	37
In Your Name	39
Carpenter's Son	40
Cry Of The Poet	42
Your Holiness	43
The Messiah	45
Christ Risen	46
P.E.S	48
Convicted	50
Resurrected	51
All Come	52
Wismatic Gesture	53
The Good Fight	54
The Apostle Paul	55
No Questions Asked	56
Hands Of Praise	57
Kingdom Keepers	59
In His Image	60
Damascus Road	61
Prodigal Son	62
Perfect Fruit	64
Reason For The Season	66

Poetic Keys to the Kingdom!
~ Third Trinity ~

The Greatest Temple Ever Created	69
Little Bittie Seed	70
He Liveth In Me	71
A Man	73
Expediency	74
Lessons	75
My Dad	76
Ma'at	77
Flashback	79
Backslider	80
God's "Do" Diligence	81
Under Pens	82
Ring Your Own Bell	83
Orphan	85
Sanctuary	87
Brother's Keeper	88
Touched By An Angel	90
More Than An Idol	91
God's Best Friend	94
What Does It Mean?	96
Metamorphosis	97
A Time To Be Born And A Time To Die	99
The Wall	101
Reader's Acknowledgment	103

Dedicated to...

My most lovely wife Tisha and closest of friends. Thanks to all of you for being there during the countless hours of self-imposed solitude.

Your patience and support afforded me the mental space needed to create and complete this long awaited project.

~~~

Preface...

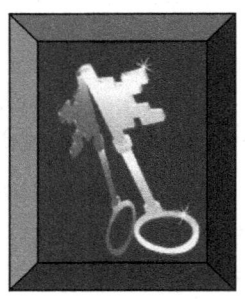

Poetic Keys to the Kingdom!

Included herein are sixty-two *"Spiritual Tablets" that are "simple poems of praise for spiritual enlightenment"*. Many of the titles find their roots in the real life experiences of the *"scribe"*, while others find their roots in the scribe's reflections on matters of *"temporal life"* and *"life eternal"*. The scribe embraces the belief that all Scriptural knowledge is the product of *"God's seeds of eternal blessing"*.

You are invited to explore this premiere publication that grew out of a larger body of works composed of prose and verse. The spiritual tablets unite poetry and Scripture in such a way that it causes the mind's eye to become open to what the Lord is saying to us in His Word. The phenomenal insight reflected in this work provides a refreshing look into the spiritual interpretation of the Word of God on a level that is simple to digest and easy to understand.

This publication was written in acknowledgment of the Holy Trinity, rendering honor, praise and glory to *God the Father, God the Son, and God the Holy Spirit*. The completed work has been brought together in a three-part composition entitled <u>*"Poetic Keys to the Kingdom : The Trinity Tablets"*</u>.

This publication serves to remind us of a commonly overlooked fact when it comes to living. So let us not forget that life with all of its intricacies has for itself the results of the experiential distance traveled, which often times is interpreted and expressed differently by those who have reached their destination. Some may view the distance traveled as a *"journey"*, wherein others might well view the distance traveled as only a *"trip"*. I believe life to be a *"journey defined by shared experiences"*, wherein the *"trip is defined by the destination sought"* and the experiential distance is often traveled alone.

Dear heavenly Father, I thank You for granting me the

sacred art of writing that was blessed upon me as a precious gift of salvation. Jesus, I thank You for steadying the course while the Holy Spirit imparted the divine wisdom, inspirational knowledge, and spiritual understanding needed to develop and complete this long awaited publication. I thank the Holy Trinity for fashioning me into a "CREATURE OF THIRST" that I might be inspired as a pupil to eat the "Holy Book" and learn of You!!!

King of kings, Lord of lords!

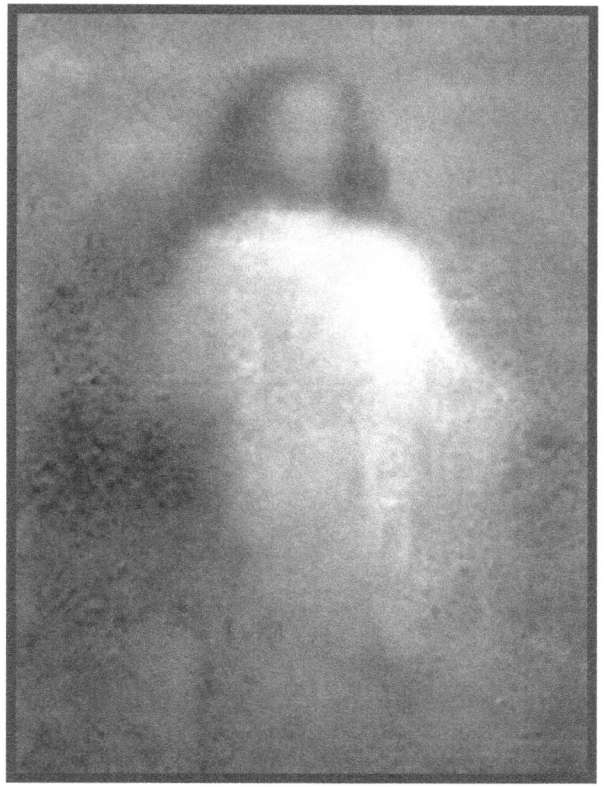

Jesus... The Key to the Holy Mystery!

"And I will give you the keys of the kingdom of heaven, and whatever you bind on earth will be bound in heaven, and whatever you loose on earth will be loosed in heaven."

Matthew 16:19 {New King James Version}

First Trinity

"Glorifying Jehovah... Our Heavenly Father!"

The Shortest Poem Ever Written...

"In the beginning...
God created the heaven
and the earth!"

Genesis 1:1 {New International Version – UK}

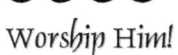

Worship Him!

The Scribe!

One who has received much!

In preparing to write this book…
I searched the breadth and depth of my being,
reminiscing back to the threshold of my conscious existence,
only to discover four things that were most prevalent to me;
the pain of *emptiness, grief, death and despair.*

It appeared as though I had witnessed
the countless faults of my life laughing out at me,
glaring out from deep within the ever widening cracks
of an ages-old looking glass.

My early life was sorely reminiscent
of a gigantic jigsaw puzzle,
one fragmented and broken into
millions and millions of assorted pieces,
only for me to receive *"last pieces first"*.

I can vividly remember being awakened
one bright and sunny April's morning…
out of what appeared to be a devil's trance,
to a myriad of voices conversing in a violent storm.

My life… once simple, respectable and good,
had become tarnished and riddled with habitual stench.
My soul was exhausted and fatigued from running,
leaving my heart paralyzed by years of reckless abandon.

I had grown aimlessly lost and totally confused,
dwelling among many of whom I no longer knew or trusted.
I was suffering from extreme paranoia and spiritual exhaustion,
brought on by my paradoxical and nonsensical existence.

Unbeknownst to myself…

I had wantonly and carelessly squandered

the greatest and most precious of life's gifts.
God's fundamental gifts of eternal blessing…
which are… love, joy, peace and happiness!

By age twenty-three, I had engaged two countries,
five states and several cities;
only to find that I could no longer escape
the haunting memories of my being.

Nonetheless, there came a time when I…
One who had consciously forsaken God,
heard, witnessed, and envisioned things
that a corrupt mind and spiritless soul could not bear.

It was here at this peaceful juncture
that I acknowledged, confessed
and accepted Jesus Christ as Lord
and Savior of my life.

Thank You heavenly Father
for my unabbreviated being,
as perceived by those whom doubted Your blessings
of earthly longevity and divine purpose in my life.

The doubts and hopes of many
concerning my life choices
would have been correct,
had it not been for Your unconditional love.

Eternal thanks to You heavenly Father
in the name of Your precious Son Jesus
for allowing Your Holy Spirit
to establish permanent residency in me!

"Scriptural Reference"
Luke 12:48

~ The Precious Present ~

Glorifying the "Heavenly Gift Giver"!

My life has been one of…
sheer essence without introduction…
Having come from humble beginnings…

Going back to a time when life was hard,
but living was simple.
A time when lessons were profound,
though rarely devastating.

Growing up during difficult moments, wherein history
when dauntingly pressed, birthed cultural heroes among us.

Being blessed to have parental giants always in our midst.
Many of whom we knew, some well acquainted
and others unknown.
Being influenced and sometimes mentored by those,
who would cause the courses of our lives to be permanently
altered.

Big and small they walked among us.
Some with a story to tell and others with just a simple sigh
that issued from a dimly fainted whisper,
only to receive an announcement in one ear…
"You have arrived"!

Going to and fro on different stages and worldly platforms,
engaging the throws of life…
In a place where choice gives way to happenstance…
Yes, you have arrived at a place of being.

A place carved out by the notions and fears
of celebrated change and new beginnings.
Being ushered into a welcoming time of arrival,
that shouts loudly… *"You are finally here"!*

<u>Here</u>, in a place of structure where there was none.
Walking with a newly secured sense of *personal pride,
self-confidence* and *"predefined purpose"*.

A place where *"Odd"* embraces *"Even"*;
wherein the oddity of pain justifies the passions
and pleasures previously misunderstood.

No longer burdened by the bonds of traditional restraints…
life takes on the challenges and beginnings of a new story.
A story to some that reads like a lullaby… that guides.

A story that changed the narrative in my life…
A story that gave me something to run from,
when I had nothing to run to.
A story that provided me with a fixed perspective,
when I had no perspective at all…

A story that granted me the gift of artful expression
and unrelenting self-persuasion…
A story that opened my heart and mind to God…
at a time when my path was twisted and dimly lit!

There's not a day goes by that I don't thank God
for my glorious and wonderful life.
A life filled with delightful pleasures without penalty.
In the Lord I've lived and experienced a colorful,
fulfilling and blessed existence.

Limitless measure and eternal thanks to…
God the Father, His Son Jesus
and the Holy Spirit, our Comforter!

I am eternally grateful for my life with all of the gifts
and treasured blessings that have been supplanted therein.
It is for this reason that I praise, honor, glorify and adore Him.

To our heavenly Father…

be the praise, the honor and the glory!

~~~

"Scriptural Reference"
James 1:16 thru 18 & Proverbs 18:15 thru 16

˜ My Name Is Spirit ˜

We shall all bear witness!

I have come only once,
but my arrivals have been many.
I have arrived in many spaces
existing behind strange and sometimes familiar faces.

For generations, centuries and millenniums…
some illusive… among others too numerous to count.
I have arrived…
many, many, times before.

My name is Spirit…

Many have witnessed My coming,
through the opening and closing of life's doors.
I have arrived…
many, many, times before.

My name is Spirit…

I have come as seasonal rain in Maine,
I have come as snow-capped mountains in Germany and Spain.
I have come as gentle breezes blowing in the Mediterranean winds.
I have arrived time and time again…

My name is Spirit…

I have come as icy lakes and frozen ponds in winter.
I have come as morning dew and misty fog in spring.
I have come as gamma rays and radiation in summer.
I have come as floral tree leaves transitioning in autumn's rain.

I have arrived… My name is Spirit!!!

"Scriptural Reference"
John 3:8, Revelation 2:7 & John 4:24

~ Rich Little ~

A parent's resistance to a son's call to salvation!

Material is loaned
it is not to be owned
it was written, so it shall be.

Man does not own
the ground he stands on
to proudly boast how powerful is he.

When a man dies
his truths becomes lies
for the whole of the world to see.

All that man owns
is his will to go on
to witness eternity.

~~~

"Scriptural Reference"
Matthew 6:19 thru 21

~ Thou Shall Not ~

Mercy unto Adam... God's "Master Creation"!

Adam made the choice
away from God he turned,
human life transformed
man's future was ruined.

For God told them
not to eat of the tree!!!

Adam looked to heaven
he was all alone,
man's earthly dominion was lost...
Eden's *"spirit culture"* was gone.

For God told them
not to eat of the tree!!!

We're commanded to obey God
by simply doing what we're told,
whether we've lived the years of Methuselah
or we're just a few years old.

For God told them
not to eat of the tree!!!

Remember Adam and Eve
God's first woman and man,
they were given special instructions
but they blew the plan.

For God told them
not to eat of the tree!!!

When they ate of the tree of knowledge of good and evil
and consumed the *essence of the fruit*,
the *"spiritual tie that binds"* was broken

and old Satan was loosed.

{Fruit eaten, but the "<u>forbidden knowledge of GOD</u>" consumed!}

For God told them
not to eat of the tree!!!

Satan encouraged Eve to eat the fruit
promised they would *"<u>be as Gods</u>"*,
not disclosing knowledge alone
only makes one smart.

For God told them
not to eat of the tree!!!

So here we are…
prisoners of SIN,
for knowledge without power
transforms *eternal mortals* into men.

For God told them
not to eat of the tree!!!

God's power is what's needed
over what we were *<u>not suppose to know</u>*,
without God's Holy Anointing
Satan is running the show.

For God told them
not to eat of the tree!!!

Jesus taught the multitude in parables
unlike His disciples to whom knowledge
of heavenly mysteries He revealed,
before being crucified on Calvary at Golgotha Hill.

For God told them
not to eat of the tree!!!

In the New Testament book of Mark,

Jesus instructed His disciples to go out and teach,
but not before receiving the *"Power Of Anointing"*
in order to practice what they preached.

{The Holy Spirit descends upon the disciples on the Day of Pentecost...}

For God told them
not to eat of the tree!!!

~~~

"Scriptural Reference"
Genesis 2:15 thru 17 & Genesis 3:12 thru 13

~ Daughters ~

Adam's love for Eve overshadows his obedience to God!

Adam flirted with death
when creation was innocent and young,
Eve gave birth to sorrow
for the old serpent she did not shun.

Death and Sorrow became partners
embracing one another madly,
procreating life's oldest set of surviving twins
"Happiness" and *"Sadness"*.

Over time the daughters grew up
went about their separate ways,
romancing the corrupt hearts of men
for the fullness of their days.

Death and Sorrow became vagabonds
wandering the dreaded pathways of life,
with little concern for man's tomorrows
or his hardships and sacrifice.

Happiness and Sadness became devoted servants
in the spiritually anointed prophetic works of God,
functioning as guardians to the blessings and curses
that prosper and damn us all.

Are you peaceful?
Are you prosperous?
Are you happy?
Choose you this day!

"Scriptural Reference"
Deuteronomy 30:19

~ I Am That I Am ~

Primal impact of Genesis chapter one, verse two!

When Spirit willed itself
to reign as ruler,
the *"Kingdom of Darkness"*
became illusion.

Spirit begot *light*,
Word begot *sound*,
Water begot *dust*,
creation abound.

World of worlds
cast from clones of never,
shrouded in lights
in a space called heaven.

Man stands in awe
of the macrocosm of space,
inflicting colossal fears
upon the entire human race.

The continuum is such....

Man's life is the *vineyard*,
Time is the *keeper*,
Christ is the *sower*,
Death is the *reaper*.

"I Am That I Am"!
I Am space and time.
I Am the Spirit of Creation.
I make the worlds go around.

I Am the Father of fathers,
I Am the maker of men.
I cause all things to die,

and come to life again.

I Am the greenness of grass,
I Am the fullness of season.
I Am soundness of mind,
I Am ration and reason.

"I Am That I Am",
God of life and life to come.
I Am the many of many,
yet I am one.

Seek ye my Spirit,
I Am balance and truth.
I Am the beginning and the end.
I Am also you!

"Scriptural Reference"
Genesis 1:1 thru 2 & 1st John 5:6 thru 8

~ Divine Purpose ~

Sanctification of the Christian Church!

For 6,000 blessed years
through the triumphs and the fears,
God You never left us…
You promised, we trusted, You kept us!

Beginning with the patriarch Abraham
whom You made *"Father of many nations"*,
we were blessed with Your divine deliverance
in and out of every hopeless situation.

Under Your prophetic guidance
and personalized direction,
the Children of Israel increased and survived
400 years of Egypt's enslavement and dejection.

Around the year 1491 B.C.
You forced Pharaoh to set the children of Israel free,
during a forty years sojourn in the wilderness
You said to Moses… "Prove Me"!

An estimated two million Hebrew children
with Pharaoh breathing down their backs,
You imparted Your *vision, plan,* and *purpose*
until today the Christian Church has not looked back.

You dedicated thirteen apostles, including Paul
dressed them in the full armor of God
charging them to proclaim liberty to the captives
wherein the faithful were divinely set apart.

Now more than thirty-six hundred years later
Christians number two billion believers strong,
boldly invading the gates of hell
emulating the praise of King David in the Psalms.

Poetic Keys to the Kingdom!

Just another chapter in an awesome story
so meticulously and eloquently told
of how God uses imperfect people
to take back what Satan stole.

~~~

"Scriptural Reference"
Hebrews 3:4 thru 11

~ Seven Seals ~

To Jesus Christ the Divine Revelator!

Passionate cries igniting static winds
here and now *"Revelation"* begins.

Crippling waves weaving woes undone
"Great Opener of Seals" Your time has come.

The prophetic events that St. John did not write
manifesting themselves in the darkness of light.

Day by day increasing agony and fear
in sea, air and earth we are dying here.

Nature is reeling from ecological harm
sounding echoes and tremors of environmental alarm.

Heavenly Host, Sweet Majesty of grace and charm,
messenger of tsunamis, quakes, fires and crop circles
freely sound Your alarms.

The Spirit of God
that once cradled the religions of man
has since glorified the Father in His *"Master Plan"*.

A symbol of sacrifice we have, crowning our partition of hope
thus striking life's pendulum in the Earth's hour of revolt.

Old *"Mother of Dust"* please absorb the shocks
until Christ's second coming You're all we've got.

"Scriptural Reference"
Revelations 5:4 thru 6

~ Babylon ~

Last days phenomenon!

Lost ties... weeping eyes,
chains of bondage in disguise.
Meek flesh melting... melting fast,
melting like hot wax on charcoal bones
avenging the wrath of the rich man's throne.

Fun, folly, drink and play
celebrating scores of yesterday.

But nobody cares to hear!!!

Eyes... brown, blue, gray and green
witnessing things they've never dreamed.
Lips thin... thick..., moving super slick,
while our lives flow like wine...
being free of purpose and free of time.

Knowingly making our children drunk for the world,
while drowning them in empty promises of yesterday.

But nobody cares to hear!!!

While living in a world filled with miseries and fears,
the fear of what was... shaping the misery of what is.

But nobody cares to hear!!!

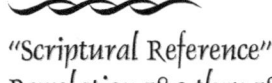

"Scriptural Reference"
Revelation 18:9 thru 18

~ Mother Love ~

In search of a bride!

All the trials of wicked men
have risen to defeat,
their conscience knows of nothing
but the remnants of deceit.

Good old Mother Nature
bless peace upon the land,
You've labored long and unceasingly
since your relationship with man.

I thank You for the morning,
the wake of everyday...
the sun that lights the path of truth
that guides me along the way.

I thank You for the evening
when my duties are almost done;
I thank You for my will to live
to keep my thoughts as one.

Love... ole Mother Love...
where in the heavens can You be?
I have searched the wide world over
even beyond the seas.

Please give me strength to seek tomorrow
beneath a morning sky
to find a love as pure as Yours
to love until I die.

I want to thank You!

"Scriptural Reference"
Ecclesiastes 9:9 & Song of Solomon 8:7

~ Cradle Of Hope ~

Blessings of a clean heart!

If a journey to the center of the human heart was possible…
after having received Christ into one's life,
upon arrival one would surely find
the province of universal love.

a place uninhabited by feelings of fear and want…
a place filled with love, joy, peace and harmony…
a place where carnal creatures die and spiritual babes are born…
a place where hurt is rendered harmless by the power of peace…
a place where confusion is blinded by the light of understanding…

a place where pride and possession is freely surrendered…
a place where power journeys to seek compassion…
a place where coldness wanders in search of warmth…
a place where sadness awaits to bond with gladness…
a place where hatred is transformed into God's love…

A beautiful place located deep within the core of the human spirit,
where time and love when given proper space,
melts down mountains of sorrow into rivers of joy
and glimmers of hope become an eternal oneness.

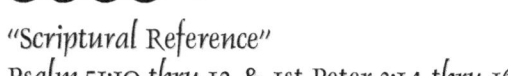

"Scriptural Reference"
Psalm 51:10 thru 12 & 1st Peter 3:14 thru 16

~ So They Say ~

The true meaning of mission?

They're on a mission from God
or so they say,
but people are sick and dying
they've lost their way.

Blessed with an abundance of food
they carelessly throw it away,
while people are hungry and starving
without a place to stay.

They live in extravagant homes
with excesses swelling their heads,
while people sleep on the street
using rocks and cardboard for beds.

Young girls on the street
fully clothed in the nude,
daily selling their innocence
just to buy food.

Little boys in bondage
held hostage by heroine, meth and crack,
while old people eat cat and dog food
to keep warm and have clothes on their backs.

They say they're on a mission
but they've been misled,
their publicly misguided charities
have gone to their heads.

They'll put thousands of dollars in church
but won't buy a homeless person a sandwich to eat,
while proudly boasting of their Christianity
to every *"perceived sinner"* they meet.

They've lost their way!

~~~~

"Scriptural Reference"
1st Corinthians 13:1 thru 2 & Matthew 5:42 thru 45

~ The Seer ~

Blood of the altar!

Where angels fly
mortals' feet can't tread,
for beneath God's altar
martyred saints bow their heads.

Piercing eyes of emerald,
cloven tongues of brass,
judgment being spoken
from Law and Prophecy's past.

Seen through the eyes
of the all-seeing Speaker!

"Scriptural Reference"
Revelation 18:24, Revelation 16:5 thru 7 & Revelation 4: 8

~ Thy Kingdom Come ~

Receiving the keys!

When I pause to view the world around me
what on Earth do I see?
Do I see the coming kingdom of God
with outstretched arms embracing me?

Do we live in a place where God's angels are welcome?
Were they to permanently come, could they relax and sing?
Or, do we live in a state of sinful existence
where God's angels couldn't spread their wings?

Have we come to a place in time
where it's illegal to call God's name?
When the words *"In God We Trust"*
boast America's claim to fame!

Have we approached a time in history
where dictators have no place?
When the God of the Ten Commandments
dictated His laws to Moses face to face *(figuratively)*.

Isn't it ironic... that *"demo"*
is the root word for democracy?
By *"majority rule"* was democracy born
when man authorized Satan to be his proxy
by eating the fruit from the forbidden tree!

"Prince of this world"... was Satan crowned
from man's thirst to equal God and be free
by casting the first *"majority vote"* in history
when Adam and Eve ate the forbidden fruit reserved for Thee.

Isn't it also ironic... that *"demo"*
is the root word for demon... *"devil in the flesh"*

reverse the English words *"live"* and *"lived"*
and the Lord may use you yet.

Ideologically correct it may seem
but in believing backwards we flunk the test,
in misunderstanding a great lesson of history and nature
that the *"East"* <u>cannot</u> be the *"West"*.

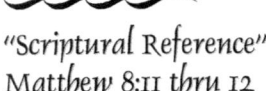

"Scriptural Reference"
Matthew 8:11 thru 12

~ You Are ~

Honoring the perpetual presence of our Creator!

Thank You Father for giving me
a face of happiness and a heart of joy,
a spirit that smiles to embrace the world.

Thank You Father for You,
for You are my blessing.
You are the air that I breathe.
You are the sun that shines.

You are infinite being, beauty, and worth... You Are!

Before light... You Are!
Before Heaven and Earth... You Are!
Before vegetation, plants and trees... You Are!

Before sun, moon, stars... You Are!
Before sea creatures, wing creatures, cattle,
creeping things, beast and man... You Are!

As stated in Revelations 3:14...
In the form of the *"...Amen, the Faithful and True Witness, the beginning of the creation of God"*... You Are!

As stated in Genesis 1:2...
Even in the mist of eternal *"Darkness"*
You were *"Spirit"* bonding with *"Water"*... You Are!

You transformed Genesis 1:2 into the *"foundation of the world"* by substituting the darkness with Your Word...
causing *"divinity of the Godhead"* to abound... You Are!

Before the Host of Heaven, angels, Satan, or hell,
You existed in the form of "The Holy Spirit"... You Are!

You are everything natural, good and life sustaining.
You are creation in its everlasting form.

Poetic Keys to the Kingdom!

That and more... You Are!

~~~

Scriptural Reference...
Colossians 1:15 thru 18

~ God Knows ~

Honoring the omniscience of our Creator!

Father we trust You…
to direct us in the ways that we should go,
for we know not our true destinies.

For in You resides the knowledge of all things!

Father we trust You…
to grant us the vision to see the heavenly for we know not how,
because we are blinded by the things that are earthly.

For in You resides the knowledge of all things!

Father we trust You…
to teach us how to pray for the things that we are in need of,
for we know not what things to ask.

For in You resides the knowledge of all things!

Father we trust You…
to instruct us in the right and perfect things to do,
for we know not what choices are best for our futures.

For in You resides the knowledge of all things!

Father we trust You…
to tell us the right and perfect things to speak,
for we know not how to govern our tongues.

For in You resides the knowledge of all things!

Father we trust You…
to reconcile our emotions with our thought lives,
for we know not how to discern the ways of the "Evil One".

For in You resides the knowledge of all things!

Father we trust You…
to balance our physical appetites with our spiritual needs,

for we know not what things are healthy and enriching for us.

For in You resides the knowledge of all things!

Father we trust You…
to guide our walk and order our steps until we are old,
for we know not which paths are best to reward our journeys.

For in You resides the knowledge of all things!

Father we trust You…
to lead us back into the face of Your presence,
for we know not how, because in Adam we have lost our way.

For in You resides the knowledge of all things!

Father we trust You…
to reestablish us in our rightful place of spiritual authority,
for we know not how because Satan has corrupted our minds.

For in You resides the knowledge of all things!

Father we trust You…
to continually remind us of whom we are in You,
it is through the indwelling of Your Holy Spirit
that we know You… the "I Am That I Am"

For in You resides the knowledge of all things!

Father we will forever glorify, honor and adore You.
It is through Your heavenly out-dwelling in Jesus Christ,
that we have come to know, love, trust and depend on You…
In whom "I Am" You Are!

For in You resides the knowledge of all things!

"Scriptural Reference"
Romans 8:26 thru 27, Proverbs 3:5 thru 7 & Isaiah 40:13 thru 14

Second Trinity

"To Jesus, God's Only Begotten Son!"

The Greatest Name Ever Spoken...

"And behold, thou shalt conceive
in your womb, and bear a son,
and you shall call His name

JESUS."

Luke 1:31 {New King James Version}

Praise Him!

~ The Adam Family ~

Eternal blessings to Sister Cynthia!

To our Lord and Savior Jesus Christ,
our High Priest, so anointed, so dear,
we render praise and honor to our heavenly Father
for His mercy in dispatching You here.

For 2000 years You have strengthened our spirits,
nurturing us with Your gospel along the way,
You have prepared the souls of many
to *"bear your cross"* day-by-day.

Many false prophets are dead and gone
only You have risen from the dead to stay,
to resurrect and guide the family of Adam
into that promised Judgment Day!

"Scriptural Reference"
Genesis 5:1 thru 2 & 1st Peter 4:17 thru 18

~ Thank You Jesus ~

I am... because You are!

I want to thank You Jesus
for all You have done for me.
I want to thank You Jesus
for setting my spirit free.

I want to thank You Jesus
for lifting me up that day.
You turned me around;
You sat me on my way.

I was lost in sin
from oh so long ago,
but You came into my life
and You told me so.

You said, listen child
There is something I'll have you do.
I have a message
I want you to take it through.

I want you to tell the world,
that I Am "The Father's" only child.
Tell them... God of Heaven sent Me here
to keep this old world alive.

Tell them... I died on Calvary
about two thousand years ago.
Tell them... I rose again the third day
to let the whole world know.

I hold the keys to death and hell
closed in the spike marks of My hands,
I have paid the eternal price
for each and every man.

Tell them… they don't have to die no more,
oh no you don't,
for the eternal price has been paid
to satisfy your every want.

Tell them… to come on in
and dine in My Father's house.
Where the *"Bread of Life"* has been broken
to feed each and every mouth.

Tell them… they are My Father's now!
Oh yes you are…
You are the seed of Abraham,
you are My Father's shining star.

You are the staff of Moses,
you are the wine from the winepress.
You are the lily of the valley,
you are My Father's very best.

Yes you are…

"Scriptural Reference"
Philippians 4:4 thru 7

~ In Your Name ~

The heavenly Father's name declared in the Earth!

Lord in Your name
we give You glory.
Lord in Your name
we share Your story.

Lord in Your name
we challenge the *"poisoned seed"*.
Lord in Your name
We are created to believe.

Lord in Your name
the Holy Spirit abounds.
Lord in Your name
lost souls are found.

Lord in Your name
we receive mercy and grace.
It is in the name of Jesus
that we have no disgrace!

Thank You dear Jesus
for You alone are worthy!

"Scriptural Reference"
Philippians 2:9 thru 11 & John 17:25 thru 27

~ Carpenter's Son ~

Knowledge is strength; strength leveraged is power!

Comfortable was I
supported by the LIE,
scared to death of living
and too afraid to die.

Treading life's edge
standing front and center,
walking the worldly walk
serving Satan's agenda.

Too busied by a world
wherein truth is denied,
I embraced the false realization
that in worldly knowledge we survive.

To God is the glory…
knowledge alone is not truth,
contrary to societal teachings
circumscribed in our youths.

Truth is "BALANCE"…
information and *knowledge* are keys,
tools used to transport us into a space
where we all can believe.

Jesus came not to the Earth to destroy
but lived and died to fulfill,
when he drank *"Adam's cup of sin and death"*
atop of Golgotha Hill.

One April's day I awoke
from the sin of spiritual death unto life,
to the teachings of *"spiritual truth"*
that only the Holy Spirit can provide.

God's *"Word"* is *"Truth"*…
Peace and Love is *"Balance"*.
The Holy Spirit sheds *"Light"*…
Jesus Christ is our example.

~~~

"Scriptural Reference"
2nd Peter 1:2 thru 4 {King James Version}

~ Cry Of The Poet ~

The anointing of the gift received!

The perfect poem
that I never wrote,
until in You Lord Jesus
I found my yoke.

Not in words
but in spiritual deeds,
the *"I Am That I Am"*
You are all I need.

Outside of sin
I have found the "TRUTH",
without Your precious love
what would I do?

Would I make a case?
Perhaps run a race?
Would I trample the kind
or embattle the human race?

O' Lord, from deep within us…
Your Spirit cries out…
"Abba" Father, "Abba" Father,
there is no doubt.

"Scriptural Reference"
Colossians 3:17, Galatians 4:4 thru 6 & Psalm 45:1

~ Your Holiness ~

The eternal light of man!

O' Holy Magnet
You are my heart's desire,
You ignite my spirit
You set my soul on fire.

You magnify my thoughts
You make me see,
the abundance of life
long buried in me.

From the days of my yearning
You heard and saw my plight,
You pricked my heart
You brought forth the "LIGHT".

Out of a sea of darkness
from whence I had come,
by Your almighty hand
a miraculous work was done.

You cleansed my soul
You established my sight,
You are the *"Messenger of Love"*
You are the Father's delight.

You are an endless breath of scripture
the everlasting illumination of men,
You shine in our hearts
and we are made to live again.

You are our power of redemption;
You surrendered Your precious life for us.
You died to redeem our souls
from Satan's wanton touch.

Poetic Keys to the Kingdom!

"Scriptural Reference"
John 1:1 thru 5 & John 1:11 thru 13

~ The Messiah ~

Promise of the coming Savior fulfilled!

Jesus is a mortal's way of dying,
He is a human's way of trying.
Jesus is man's best friend,
He is a lover of our lives
from beginning to end.

Jesus is man's extension of time.
Jesus sacrificed His life for all mankind.

Through Jesus, the Father expresses
His innermost harmonious feelings
of His love for the world.

The Spirit of Jesus is that silent force
that causes life to confess all truth.

So, let us pause and ask ourselves,
just as Pontius Pilate once asked Jesus…
What is truth?

Jesus is "THE TRUTH" of all creation!
Jesus is the "ETERNAL LIGHT" of man's salvation!
Jesus is that "GOOD SHEPHERD" that guides us…

When the brighter side of darkness
resonates like a sparkle in the sunset!

"Scriptural Reference"
John 1:35 thru 42

~ Christ Risen... ~

Beyond the breach!

Fear, hate, and schism
Jesus Christ has surely risen,
from the manger to the grave
resurrected to redeem the human race.

Three days swallowed up by the Earth
destined to fulfill the Savior's immaculate birth.
Swallowed up like Jonah in the belly of a whale
Jesus descended into the fiery depths of hell.

The *"cup of sin and death"* that Adam filled
Jesus drank to do His Father's will,
to save a bunch of sinners lives
that squandered dominion in paradise.

Rejected by His very own
Jesus walked the road to death alone,
undeterred by the religious schism
Jesus fulfilled His Father's business.

Although Lord... He calls us friends
a love hard for unredeemed sinners to comprehend,
One from whom the disciples fearfully scattered,
One in whom the Jews chose to free *"Barabbas"*.

Jesus promised a triumphant return
from Whom the mountains will flee and run,
at which time the Earth will soon discover
"there will not be one stone left upon another".

Jesus is coming back!
Every knee shall bow!
Every tongue shall confess...
that Jesus Christ is Lord!

Thus saith the Lord of Hosts!!!

"Scriptural Reference"
1st Corinthians 12:20 thru 25

~ P. E. S. ~

Miracles performed to the glory of God not Satan!

Satan's triple threat is targeting me,
it's called *"P. E. S."* ...oooh can't you see?
God's latest manifestation
of an ages old mystery.

Provocation, Enticement, Submission...
The Tempter's tools of the game,
but don't be surprised...
Satan is his name.

Satan appeals to our carnal nature...
this is crucial... check it out!
Jesus overcame three models of human weaknesses,
so there would be no doubt.

"The Spirit led Jesus out of the wilderness
to be tempted of the devil"
examine the Holy Scriptures
to understand Satan's cleverness.

"If thou be the Son of God *(Satan Said)*...
command that these stones be made bread"
Provocation.... Provocation.... Provocation....
Don't be misled!

"If thou be the Son of God *(Satan Said)*...
cast thyself down and the angels shall bear thee up"
Enticement... Enticement... Enticement...
Same old stuff!

"If thou be the Son of God *(Satan Said)*...
things will I give thee, if thou wilt fall down and worship me"
Submission... Submission... Submission...
Don't be deceived!

Miracles are performed
to the glory of God and not the devil
If Jesus had turned stones into bread,
He would have elevated Satan into Heaven.

Satan doesn't have power to destroy,
he can only spiritually disrupt.
Had Jesus cast Himself down as Satan instructed,
He would have died of suicide causing Himself to self-destruct.

The Holy Spirit is our *"Comforter"*,
He exists to instruct and guide us.
We are to submit to God only,
for in the heavenly Father we trust.

All glory be to God,
God and God alone…
The Universe is God's house.
Heaven is God's throne.

"Scriptural Reference"
Hebrews 4: 15, Ephesians 3:16 & 1st John 4:4

~ Convicted ~

Personal sacrifice... the true measure of service!

Spiritual addiction...
enduring worldly affliction,
I heard *"by His stripes we are healed"*.
Remember...

There is no conviction... without suffering!

From within the Lamb's Book of Life,
Jesus is our eternal sacrifice.
Hear Him...

There is no conviction... without suffering!

The prison of life poses no earthly escape,
for this reason Jesus became a death row inmate.
"Choose ye this day..."

There is no conviction... without suffering!

To receive "abundant life"
we must deny ourselves.
In God we survive and are spiritually kept...

There is no conviction, without suffering!

Jesus and His apostles endured the tests,
by surrendering their lives.
We must never forget...

There is no conviction... without suffering!

"Scriptural Reference"
1st Peter 4:12 thru 14 & Colossians 1:23 thru 24

~ Resurrected ~

God of the eternal awakening!

You are the reason why
I did not die,
You called me out
I cannot deny.

You brought me back
You made me see,
those spiritual truths
born dead in me.

Like biblical Lazarus
from sleep I awoke,
stepped out of my sin
cast down my yoke.

I heard Your knock,
the *"WORD"* transformed my life,
You revealed *"The Truth"*
in You I survive.

You are justified dear Lord
to hold the key,
You pleased our heavenly Father
when You died for me.

A worthless sinner was I
before You saved my soul,
You are my *"Living Testimony"*
a story worthy to behold.

"Scriptural Reference"
Romans 8:10 thru 11

~ All Come ~

Accepting redemption!

Everlasting life, abundant and free
surrender your heart and soul and freely eat,
Christ's Word when eaten
is spiritual food for meat.

By the shedding of the Lamb's blood
unto the heavenly Father we are called,
every race, sex, creed and color
come one, come all!

The door to redemption,
salvation and eternal life
is open…
All come!

"Scriptural Reference"
Revelation 22:14 thru 17 & Matthew 11:28 thru 30

~ Wismatic Gesture ~

Finding the inner path!

People that continuously walk
forever watching their feet,
blindly trip over the mistakes of others
that contributes to their defeat.

Rough roads are seldom traveled
discouraging bumps they do possess,
the *"chosen"* and *"faithful"* are servants
unto sacrifice, wherein Christ we find our rest.

"Scriptural Reference"
1st Peter 2:7 thru 9 & Psalm 16:9 thru 11

~ The Good Fight ~

On the right side of Right!

Although some are rich
and many are poor,
there is one simple truth
that all should know.

When it comes to life
be it wrong or right,
we are commanded to stay the course
and fight the *"good fight"*.

Be we weak or strong
against thick or thin,
trust in the power of God
and not in the traditions of men.

The righteous were chosen
even before time began,
keep your hope and faith in Jesus
until the very end.

"Fight the good fight"

"Scriptural Reference"
1st Timothy 6:11 thru 12 & Colossians 2:8

~ The Apostle Paul ~

The apostle of the Gentiles!

The Holy Scriptures record
that during the days of old,
Jesus anointed a persecutor of Christians
to preach the gospel of Christ
who was exceedingly bold.

He was Saul of Tarsus
a very zealous and learneth man,
a devout disciple of the law of Moses
before taking a righteous stand.

God struck a zealous murderer blind
to allow the renowned Apostle Paul to see,
how the crucifixion of the *"Lamb of God"*
would set the whole of humanity free.

~~~~~

"Scriptural Reference"
Acts 8:1 thru 3 & Romans 1:1

~ No Questions Asked ~

Jack Eugene Walker... My guiding light to Christ!

When I look to my past,
and think of my life;
I am reminded of the perfect love of Jesus,
and *"His ultimate sacrifice"*.

Born into a cash driven world,
moving much too fast;
I was not surprised to find...
that I was wearing a mask.

From beyond the veil,
I was permitted a glimpse...
of *"the Lamb"* appointed to die,
One in Whom the world would deny.

Before my relationship with Christ,
my life was simply a token...
superficially camouflaged,
mis-managed and severely broken.

Completely void beyond measure,
I had forfeited every treasure,
until with a peaceful voice I clashed,
hearing... *"There are no questions asked"*.

"Scriptural Reference"
John 10:27 thru 28 & 2nd Peter 1:17 thru 18

~ Hands Of Praise ~

Blessed be Havaughnia!

From You Holy Father
I received believing hands of praise,
that emulates Your power and glory
in a myriad of ways.

Not stagnant hands
that do not fashion or build,
but resourceful hands
empowered with creativity and skill.

Hands that when pressed
meet the heavenly Father's mark,
adorned to bless
and touch the broken hearted.

Hands that heal
to mend shattered lives,
hands that have endured suffering
and have been deprived.

Hands that are worthy…
in Your Son they are blessed,
hands that are highly favored
to withstand every test.

Father it is with these hands
that I give You honor and glory;
Father it is with these hands
that I inscribe Your story.

Father it is from within the hollow of Your hands
that I have received spiritual touch.
By Your hands was my life made eternal
and granted spiritual worth.

Father, it is with these hands
that I give You the highest praise;
For by the works of Your mighty hands
were all things created that are made.

You are worthy!

"Scriptural Reference"
Isaiah 40:10 thru 12

~ Kingdom Keepers ~

Doing what Christians do!

We were born to be believers,
We are here to take a stand,
talking about God's mercy
and His grace toward every man.

Speaking to all nations,
living witnesses of God's truth,
rendering praise, honor and glory
as we do what Christians do.

Lord we adore, honor, and love You
because You are God all alone.
We humble ourselves in Your presence
and commit our lives to Your heavenly throne!

"Scriptural Reference"
Psalm 47:7 thru 8 & Matthew 24:14

~ In His Image ~

God is man's mirror!

The mirrors of life
are the windows of the soul
through which all great truths are seen.

How can we
being blind of God and ourselves
witness what we've not dreamed?

Dreams manifest life's possibilities
unimaginably small and great,
issuing from the Creator of all visible and invisible things,
whose blessings we cannot predate.

Man is a reflection of God's image
illuminating spiritual gifts within ourselves,
a human copy of our heavenly Creator
fashioned in the image and likeness of God Himself.

Ask what you will in the name of Jesus
and let God the Father prove you this day,
we receive not because we ask not…
Jesus Christ is our heavenly Advocate!

Know your purpose…
Live your dreams…

"Scriptural Reference"
Genesis 1:27, Mark 11:24 & John 16:24 thru 25

~ Damascus Road ~

The road seldom traveled!

As I walk the roads of life,
projecting an image for all to see,
do they see a lantern of God,
that Jesus established in me?

Or do they see a gaping black hole,
all dressed and decked in stone;
Or do they see an aging body
constructed of dead dry bones?

Or do they see a Christ-like victor?
An overcomer in the trials of life,
having faithfully run the race against Satan,
while enduring life's challenges with a smile.

In the light of my eternal eye,
the Lord has made me be…
what He desires in each of us
a blinding light for all to see.

"Scriptural Reference"
Acts 22:6 thru 11 & Acts 13:9

~ Prodigal Son ~

Welcome home…!

Don't be shocked or disturbed
by what you see...
Jesus wasn't just beaten, stabbed and wounded,
please hear my plea!

He was hated and rejected by a world
that turned its back on you and me.
Thank You heavenly Father
for having mercy upon me!

Many are enraged by the horrible thoughts
of Jesus' bloody, tattered stains,
not realizing that humanity is the *"Prodigal Son"*
and old Satan is the blame.

I took the treasures of God's goodness
that were abundantly bestowed upon me,
and carelessly sowed them to the wind
for the entire world to see.

After having fallen down spiritually,
totally broken in despair,
Satan whispered in my ear…
"Eat the slop, nobody cares!"

I knew that he was lying,
for in my heart of hearts I could spiritually see,
Jesus standing wounded on life's road,
with outstretched arms awaiting me.

I tearfully looked into the eyes of my Lord…
His head pricked and punctured by a crown of thorns!
His hands spiked and dripping with blood!
His garment blooded, tattered, and torn!

His ribs pierced by the sword of a Roman soldier!
Abandoned by His disciples to die alone,
Jesus unselfishly rushed down from Calvary's cross
to personally welcome me home.

Jesus, the human manifestation of the Father
and I the spiritual *"prodigal son"*,
one who threw away his purchased inheritance
by turning away from God's only begotten Son.

Thank you dear Jesus for understanding,
You promised You would never forget my name;
You are the... *"lamb slain from the foundation of the world"*
and resurrected from the grave to bare my shame.

I know for years that I have been slack,
There is nothing justified I can possibly say,
but thank You my Holy Jesus
for receiving me back into Your kingdom to stay.

Welcome home my child... welcome home!

"Scriptural Reference"
Luke 15:11 thru 19

~ Perfect Fruit ~

The "Alpha and Omega"!

Dear Jesus…

You are the Father's perfect fruit
from life's spiritual family tree,
from within the Garden of Eden
You were reserved for all to eat.

In crucifixion You were planted
a tree of eternal life to be,
in salvation and communion
You are eaten to be free.

There is nothing more majestic
beneath heaven, earth, nor sea,
than You my Holy Jesus
You lived and died for me.

Long generations ago
in an era long gone past,
You fulfilled the sacred *"Laws of Moses"*
that seeded our sinful past.

You are the blessed *"Ten Commandments"*
the anatomy of the unborn Christ,
You are the vows of the Christian Church
Your consecrated *"Holy Bride"*.

Born in a manger
You became living Scriptures of flesh,
You are the key to the *"Holy Mystery"*
in Your name we all are blessed.

From the works of Your Father's hands
we were shaped of earthen clay,
in Your divine *"Image and Likeness"*

we live justified day-by-day.

Perfect Fruit…

~~~~

"Scriptural Reference"
John 15:1 thru 8

~ Reason For The Season ~

A Holy Child is born!

When I pause to celebrate Christmas,
realizing what Jesus means to me,
I am reminded of our resurrected Lord and Savior,
innocently crucified and left dying on a tree.

With limp body idly suspended...
pierced arms spiked and nailed outstretched;
Jesus Christ surrendered His glorious life,
to expunge humanity's every debt.

When I look to the hills of Calvary,
I am reminded of an image of a bloodied cross;
assembled vertically and horizontally,
crisscrossed and fashioned for us all.

Christ is the essence of the *"Holy Season"*,
celebrating the immaculate birth of the baby Jesus,
for without the life, death and resurrection of our Lord,
December 25th would be a day without a cause.

Satan's double-cross for the world today...
is tailored for those who have lost their way;
Every Christian should take a bold stand and say...
No Christ... No Christmas... No Holy Day!

From 2000 years ago in Bethlehem,
to Calvary throughout the world today...
Jesus is the one and only Lord and Savior,
and Christmas is here to stay!!!

No Christ, No Christmas, No Holy Day!

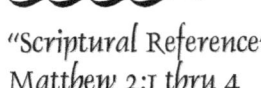

"Scriptural Reference"
Matthew 2:1 thru 4

Third Trinity

"In Honor Of Our Comforter... The Holy Spirit!"

The Greatest Temple Ever Created...

"Do you not know that your body is
a temple of the Holy Spirit, who is in you,
whom you have received from God?
You are not your own;"

1st Corinthians 6:19 {New International Version – UK}

Follow Him!

~ Little Bittie Seed ~

Eternal friend and brother... Paul Daniels!

From within the shadow of a thought
i was only a seed, simply living to be sown,
but by and by my life corrupted
i was stranded all alone.

The other seeds all scattered about
to be sown wherever they lay,
there i was alone and trapped,
ensnared by deeds of yesterday.

But all of a sudden my life sprang open
i was moved by words on high,
i was carried away to a beautiful place
and left not to die.

By what fate could it be
that i grow so tall and strong,
when all the seeds ahead of me
grew so infinitely wrong.

Could it be that a gracious God
is so resourceful and so rich,
that He causes a seed to bloom and blossom
that was gathered from a ditch.

"Scriptural Reference"
Matthew 13:3 thru 8 & Matthew 17:20

~ He Liveth In Me ~

The spiritual abode?

Inside me He speaks!
Inside me He weeps!
He whispers
a midmorning prayer.

As I gaze out upon the world
I see through His eyes,
as I witness human suffering
inside me He dies...

He lives in me!

Inside me He screams
as He chases the money changers out,
those who bring filth to the human temple
our Lord's flesh and blood house.

More silent than a rose
He came like a thief,
more passionate than a priest
He made peace within me.

He lives in me!

Like the feel of hot lava
tracing upon earthen clay,
He flowed into my life
He reshaped me that way.

An old dust bag was I
right from the start,
until the love of Jesus Christ
invaded my heart.

He lives in me!

I am in Him...
He is in me...
He's in the Father...
we all agree...

He lives in me!

~~~

"Scriptural Reference"
1st John 4:12 thru 13 & 1st Corinthians 6:19 thru 20

~ A Man ~

An island not unto itself!

I was taught my lessons as a child
only to learn them as a man.

When shall I ever learn?

A man is a grain…
he's just like sand…
he's moved by the weight of the world.

He could be a boulder if he would,
he would be a mountain if he could,
but after all… he's only a grain!

A man!

"Scriptural Reference"
1st Corinthians 13:11 & Psalm 1:1 thru 3

~ Expediency ~

Disclosing destiny's key!

In a mood of expediency
we rush to live our lives,
only to become so involved in living
that we merely learn to survive.

We take the wildest chances
seeking fun and fortune in our youth,
by repeating the errors of the fallen
we fail to know the truth.

We focus our views of yesterday
through a lens with frozen eyes,
embellishing shattered visions…
of success unrealized.

From the depths of our decisions
we create our space,
by exercising spiritual execution,
we secure our place.

Success is an unwritten formula
that the Holy Spirit within us creates,
when God is granted control of our schedules
we become "Masters" of our fate.

"Scriptural Reference"
Psalm 25:7 thru 10

~ Lessons ~

The world is our classroom... the Lord is our teacher!

Not long ago when parents were parents
and kids were kids...
We earned what we learned!
We believed in what we did!

Unlike today
when few really care,
Heaven help us all
we have lost ourselves.

Mistakes are poor choices
resulting in valuable lessons learned,
we must revisit life's errors
from whence our futures are exhumed.

From our trials come the testimonies
about which I solemnly speak,
witnessed in the presence of the Holy Spirit
which are never to be repeated.

Recounting the trials and tests
that we have experienced and overcome,
empowers our resolve for spiritual healing
until the race for salvation is run.

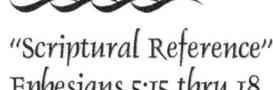

"Scriptural Reference"
Ephesians 5:15 thru 18

~ My Dad ~

A gift from my father!

"Sixty Eight"… that's great!
Thank God, Oh what a break,
it is through you that I live today.
Thanks dad… you're special!

Now that I am older
remembering all you told me;
you taught me quite a lot,
I owe you all I've got.

You are truly a remarkable man,
having done the best you can;
assuming a positive stand,
you left me the "Master Plan".

For all the days I live,
in your precious shadow
I'll plan, I'll build.
Oh what a life worth living!

I thank God for your giving,
I am truly blessed among the living.
Unlike many I have a lot,
You have granted me the "Master Slot".

You are more than great.
You are better than wonderful.
It is in you…
that I found my godly example!

Departed December 1, 1990

"Scriptural Reference"
Proverbs 1:7 thru 8 & Proverbs 23:24

~ Ma`at ~

A message from Margarita!

I speak with conviction
knowing life is a song,
all God's children
hum along, hum along.

Life is a symphony
composed of spiritual truths,
vibrating rhythmic expressions
and earthly harmonies to you.

Lift your voices
shout blessings of praise,
sing melodies of love
Heaven's chorus will play.

Be a trumpeter like the angel Gabriel
proclaim life's blessings with a shout,
sound crescendos of love
until the *"Good News"* comes out.

There is a universal principle
bridging God and man,
it is a spiritual investment
upon which Heaven depends.

We all get back
what we ourselves put in,
the measure has been the same
since time began.

We pay once going
or twice coming back,
like repetitive beats in timing
it's a natural fact.

I speak with conviction
knowing life is a song,
all God's children
hum along, hum along.

~~~

"Scriptural Reference"
Ephesians 5:19 thru 20 & Colossians 3:15 thru 16

~ Flashback ~

Divine principle of stewardship!

The aftermath of life's
most critical instructions,
becomes the consequences
of duties… completed,
or simply left undone.

Discover your purpose!
Finish your assignments!
Live your dreams!
Do it now!

"Scriptural Reference"
John 9:4

~ Backslider ~

A house built on sand!

I am, I want,
I might, I should.
If I would, I could, so I'd be.

But since I can't,
I aint… in all my trials.
I'll tell you just what I'll be.

I am what I am,
that's all I am.
What else can I possibly be?

At times I will…
At times I won't…
After all I'm only me!

"Scriptural Reference"
Proverbs 14:14, Jeremiah 3:14 & Revelation 3:16

~ God's "Do" Diligence ~

A work in progress!

Thank You Father
for loving me enough
to do all that You have done…
for me!

Thank You Jesus
for being patient enough
to do what You've done…
with me!

Thank You Holy Spirit
for being devoted enough
to do what You are doing…
in me!

"Scriptural Reference"
Colossians 2:8 thru 14

~ Under Pens ~

Life's mimicry of worldly illusion!

What poor people regard as homes
rich people view as pens,
domestic confinements for preparation
before being sent forth to work again.

While common people live like swine
in a society casting pearls at the wealthy's feet,
the poor are consuming culinary slop
while boasting of the delicacies they eat.

Do you ever sit alone and wonder
will I ever get out of this mess,
while the well-off live like royalty
and you're always struggling to be blessed.

We are children of the most-high God,
the Father of blessings from on high,
He promised to prosper all the days our lives
if in His commandments we trust and abide.

Embrace the teachings of Jesus,
the "Holy Bible" is your companion guide,
acknowledge the Holy Spirit as your eternal witness,
and all of your needs will be satisfied!

"Scriptural Reference"
Luke 18:18, Luke 18:24 thru 25 & Matthew 7:6

~ Ring Your Own Bell ~

It begins with God and ends with you!

Ain't gonna get out of bed
nor comb my hair;
Ain't gonna look my best
cause nobody cares!

Ain't gonna wash my face
nor brush my teeth;
Ain't gonna offer up praise
cause I ain't got expensive food to eat!

Ain't gonna read my Bible
nor say my prayers;
Ain't gonna go to church
cause nobody cares!

Ain't gonna clean my house
nor wash my sheets;
Ain't gonna worship the Lord
cause I ain't got new shoes on my feet!

I have searched life's mirror
surviving from day to day;
until I saw the face of a stranger
who had lost his way!

Today I've vowed in my heart
to look beyond pride and despair;
I now praise and worship the Lord
for giving me the reason to care.

Ring-A-Ding... Ding!

"Scriptural Reference"
Psalms 23:1 thru 6

~ Orphan ~

Fannie Mae... Mother-in-law, mom & friend!

As an unredeemed sinner
I lived life on Earth alone,
akin to a wandering gypsy
without the comforts home.

Dwelling deep-down without cover
or the Lord's promised daily bread,
unaware of God's everlasting *"mercy"*
and His wondrous *"grace"* ahead.

I know now with total assurance
that my *"heavenly Father"* truly lives,
in a house filled with heavenly mansions
currently existing... but not yet revealed.

I once lived unbelievably small
because I had not yet been told,
of an eternal city gated with pearls
with streets paved in gold.

Heaven is my future home
and I am yearning to go there,
to live forever in total peace
without concern, worry or care.

I long to dwell for eternity
with my long-awaited spiritual kin,
in a place free of disease...
poverty, hate and sin.

Heaven doesn't have embalmers
there aren't any doctors or nurses there,
because people live forever
and there's no need for medical care.

The Church is my spiritual family
and I'm no longer alone or ashamed,
for I am now a child of *"The Master"*
and I live in Jesus' name.

Jesus... Jesus... Jesus...

"Scriptural Reference"
Ephesians 1:3 thru 5, John 14:2 thru 3 & Revelation 2:17

~ Sanctuary ~

The promised abode!

For years in sin I freely lived
praying to God for peace revealed,
a solitary place deep inside my head
trusting in God for what lie ahead.

Blessed with mercy and grace unknown
I sensed the presence of life reborn,
until my brush with Christ I could not see
the treasure of eternal life residing in me.

Cherished sins once engaged I could not do
telling actions now clear in final review,
a hedge surrounded my life by God was placed
guaranteeing the heavenly sanctum that would await.

Amazing enough,
all of life's roads led here…
paved in the blood of Jesus Christ
in whom I honor and revere.

"Scriptural Reference"
St. John 14:21 thru 23

~ Brother's Keeper ~

Brother to brother!

Why should I grope in darkness
continuing to bare my soul?
While surrendering my blessings,
guaranteeing you total control.

I am sick and tired of sweating tears
bleeding anguish, blood, and guts;
while living in a world of plenty,
where enough... is not enough.

We are all God's children,
or don't you solemnly agree?
The character and intellect embodied in you
was created abundantly in me.

So, I ask the brotherly question...
Who on Earth do you think you are?
Are you truly my spiritual brother?
Or is your Christianity... simply a farce?

Receive this truth as a warning,
be not culturally or spiritually deceived.
You cannot be in *"right relationship"* with God
when you are in *"wrong relationship"* with me.

In the image and likeness of the Creator am I,
exceeding every creature in the earth, air and sea,
be it known that God's character and image is abused
when you knowingly mistreat me.

I am a beloved child of the Creator,
the one and only "I Am That I Am";
to those who disobey this commandment...
you are spiritually and eternally damned!

"Scriptural Reference"
1st John 4:18 thru 21 & Mark 12:28 thru 31

~ Touched By An Angels ~

An awakening from Jangel!

Even the most loyal of angels,
having ever come my way;
were creatures fashioned for elevation,
predestined to eloquently fly away.

They ascend to the greatest pinnacles,
transcending the loftiest and highest of heights;
as they gracefully spread their wings,
in wondrous and sheer delight.

You are certainly akin to those creatures,
the world knows it without doubt to be true;
The strength of GOD'S HEAVENLY CHARACTER,
is His "IMAGE" and "LIKENESS" in you.

May you always trust and believe...
in what the Lord has commanded for you;
Christ Jesus paid the price on Calvary,
for wings that are especially fitted for you!

Satan would have us believe as caterpillars...
that we can only grope, quiver and crawl...
when in the Holy Spirit we are "BLESSED & ANOINTED"
to spread our Spiritual wings and rise above it all.

"Scriptural Reference"
Hebrews 13:2 & 1st Corinthians 6:2 thru 3

~ More Than An Idol ~

Shattered vision... broken pieces!

As sinners we present ourselves,
humbled by Your holiness...
sacrificing our vanity...
surrendering our personal pride.

We stand unafraid...
trusting as little children...
agreeing to deny ourselves in order to grow,
unashamed to proudly say...
"Heavenly Father, in You I know".

When it comes to perpetrators...
there are many of whom we've known,
that have presented themselves as Christians,
whom were less than disciples or saints.

Ones who have shared...
a corrupt and vile brand of theology.
Therefore, we examine the Holy Scriptures...
and we tremble in the face of "Your WORD".

Father... it was in April of 1974,
that You drew me to a small,
white steeple church on Saragossa Street
in the downtown area of Pensacola, Florida.
It was here at this peaceful place,
that You whispered in my ear...

"Get up and speak!"

If it had not been for You...
I would have self destructed long ago...
and died a miserable death in sin,
but you were faithful toward me.

You saved me!

Dear heavenly Father I thank You,
if it were not for Your Son Jesus being on my side,
I would have been in jail or dead decades ago
awaiting the slam of the prison door
or the fiery flames of hell's fire.

Thanks to the divine knowledge magnified in Your Word,
tribulation and hardship has become a motivation;
I now understand that there is no conviction without suffering,
and I yearn to see Your face!

Christ Jesus has taught me how to
physically bend and not spiritually break
and still have the resolve to love my adversaries,
even when faced with the greatest of trials and adversity!

Therefore, I stand tall supported by
the promised assurance of Your love.
When things look doubtful
I've learned to pray and not fear...
because I know that I am a blessed child of the "Master".

Lord, it is Your kingdom that I seek,
and Your Word that I struggle to obey...
realizing daily that yielding is not easy,
I release and submit myself to You.

I need Thee O' Father!
It is within thy Spirit that I have belonging...
and in thy presence that I know no waste,
You are my rock and my tower.

A carnal babe was I,
born into a world preordained by Satan
to become a human idol prone to self-worship.

This was me before being spiritually broken,
prior to my being blessed to become a disciple of Your Word.
Thank You Father for being the potter,
and allowing life to be the wheel.

You've continuously turned me
around, and around, and around...
in the hollow of Your hand
that I might live.

Unto You almighty God I give the honor,
realizing that Your *"Might"* is the presence of Your *"Power"*.
Unto You dear Father I give the glory
knowing that Your *"Glory"* is the power of Your *"Presence"*.

Dear Father in the name of Your Son Jesus,
our Redeemer, Lord and Savior...

I thank You!

I thank You for divine citizenship
in Your glorious heavenly kingdom
that is destined to reign on Earth
for eternity!

"Scriptural Reference"
2nd Colossians 6:16 & Luke 20:17 thru 18

~ God's Best Friend ~

The greatest love affair!

They say I am dying...
but I say they are lying,
because I know...
I am God's best friend!

They say I only have months to live,
but I know that time is not theirs to give,
because I know...
I am God's best friend!

When I heard the news,
I fell on my knees and prayed...
not believing a word they had to say,
because I know...
I am God's best friend!

They told me that my end was finally here,
but my mind and heart was very clear.
because I know...
I am God's best friend!

I just could not see myself dying there,
sitting in that old hollow chair,
because I know...
I am God's best friend!

Today I embrace a life filled with cheer,
my life is in God's hand... I have no fear,
because I know...
I am God's best friend!

So on this day I say to you,
believe every word that God says is true.
We have to know...

We are God's best friend!

In God there is no death there is only life,
to this end Jesus became our human sacrifice.
For this we know…
We are God's best friend!

To believe Him,
is to receive Him…
We are truly God's best friend!

~~~

"Scriptural Reference"
John 15:12 thru 16

~ What Does It Mean? ~

In search of the eternal answer!

Rose pedicels, rainbows,
mixed feelings of a dream,
purple passion lollipops
just what does it mean?

Shades of aqua, purple, lavender and gold
draping the emotional walls of ambivalent souls.
Blue, red, yellow, orange and green,
ambient solace, just what does it mean?

Sullen smiles on beautiful faces
feelings of sadness, so out of place.
For Christ did die, shall GOD deny?
Jesus resurrected from the dead; is the WORD a lie?

In a manner of speaking
the race has been run.
No more... cap pistols,
Barbie Dolls and bubble gum.

Counting the hours
while chasing the dream,
life is a vapor
just what does it mean?

"Scriptural Reference"
James 4:13 thru 15 & 1st John 5:11 thru 13

~ Metamorphosis ~

Mystery of mysteries!

As a soul I live
as a body I die,
I spread my wings
like a butterfly.

As a cocoon I come
into life this way,
much like larva
not here to stay.

The cocoon is body,
the larva is soul,
the butterfly is life
in its spiritual mode.

Man was created mortal
formed from dust of the earth,
given the breath of life
in measured reserve.

Much like larva
given hidden wings to fly,
a creature of destiny
bound to die.

It is in deed God's purpose
that all should understand
that in life lie the mystery
not in the death of man.

Man is not to confuse
life's *"package"* with the *"gift"*,
in joy the package should be opened,
the gift a treasure to be missed.

The Spirit is the gift
wrapped in the body of man,
being explained in the Holy Scriptures
for all to understand.

Once the physical package is opened
the soul sprouts wings and flies,
soaring back into the kingdom
where it becomes immortalized.

Fly hard and long my beautiful
as you always flew for me,
as you spread your wings of love
may your shadow smile on me.

"Scriptural Reference"
1st Corinthians 15:50 thru 57

~ A Time To Be Born And A Time To Die ~

My mom... she sleepeth!

Weepeth not...
O' gentle one!
The *"last trump"* has sounded...
the time has come!

The heavenly hosts have been summoned,
the honored guests are here.
The earthly hourglass has emptied,
but have no fear.

The bridesmaids have entered,
even the dead and resurrected have arrived.
The Bridegroom *("Christ")* has appeared
to receive His adorned Holy Bride *("The Church")*.

The table of eternity has been set...
The heavenly throne is revealed...
Judgment has come down...
to weigh the deeds of our years.

Make no amends or excuses now,
for the time has past gone to sort it out.
Sleep peaceful and gently in thy day of rest,
lay thy weary head upon God's eternal breast.

Birth is an appointment made!
Death an appointment kept!
Jesus drank *"Adam's cup of sin and death"*
after He prayed and wept!

The morning star that once shined
has finally dimmed its light,
far beyond the celestial horizon
one sleeps tonight.

God's angels are smiling...
in hopes that you've done your best.
The Holy Spirit is our Teacher...
did you pass the test?

The light of day is gone
the sun is permanently at rest,
no more time to labor,
life's wages are set.

Awake...
and see His face!

"Scriptural Reference"
Ecclesiastes 3:1 thru 2, Revelation 22:10 thru 12 & Isaiah 38:18

~ The Wall ~

The greatest of life's mysteries decoded!

From out of the womb
into a crowded tunnel I came,
brandishing the thought
of becoming a man.

From among the talented and gifted
I was given a call,
being counted truly blessed
to touch the wall.

For all can see…
though only the talented can touch,
God's earthly mural that is prepared,
to speak to us.

Out of the darkness…
from water and Spirit I have come,
traveling life's tunnel
until God's work is done.

A great mystery of life
embraces and eludes us all,
why does God allow only the gifted
to touch the wall?

The wall of humanity
written on for all to see,
though only God's personal elect
can write on it.

A glimpse, touch, or feel
is but a morsel to the taste,
of what the writing will reveal
to the entire human race.

There is one whom has come
to *steal, kill and destroy*,
he paints the wall with blasphemous graffiti
after he has taken away our joy.

There is another whom spiritually dares us
to diligently look upon the wall,
to search out and understand the mystery
that confounds and saves us all.

Life is the tunnel
communicating an awesome story told,
decipher the meaning of the wall
let the writing save your soul.

At life's end there is a luminance
that exists to translate all of us,
interpret the meaning of the wall
and be translated from the dust.

Christ Jesus is the mystery…
once hidden…, now revealed!

"Scriptural Reference"
Daniel 5:5 thru 7 & Romans 16:25 thru 26

*On behalf of Neo Nexus Publishing, LLC
I personally thank you for investing
your time, energy and resource
into the exploration of...*

"Poetic Keys to the Kingdom! : The Trinity Tablets"

*I sincerely hope that you were spiritually enriched.
You are cordially invited to explore and enjoy
the future publications that are yet to come!*

Charles E. Dickerson

www.ingramcontent.com/pod-product-compliance
Lightning Source LLC
Chambersburg PA
CBHW031451040426
42444CB00007B/1055